ANCHOR BOOKS

DAYDREAM POETS

Edited by

Heather Killingray

First published in Great Britain in 1999 by
ANCHOR BOOKS
Remus House,
Coltsfoot Drive,
Woodston,
Peterborough, PE2 9JX
Telephone (01733) 898101

HB ISBN 1 85930 619 5
SB ISBN 1 85930 614 4

FOREWORD

Anchor Books is a small press, established in 1992, with the aim of promoting readable poetry to as wide an audience as possible.

We hope to establish an outlet for writers of poetry who may have struggled to see their work in print.

The poems presented here have been selected from many entries. Editing proved to be a difficult task and as the Editor, the final selection was mine.

I trust this selection will delight and please the authors and all those who enjoy reading poetry.

Heather Killingray
Editor

CONTENTS

PUT PEN TO PAPER

The written words a powerful thing.
Be it a poem, or something to sing.
It reaches people far and wide,
and shows the feelings we often hide.

If everyone wrote down their thoughts,
many lessons could be taught.
We could teach each other how to care,
and learn the art of being there.

If we all put pen to paper,
and let the writing flow.
All the thoughts inside our minds,
would soon begin to grow.

The world would be
a better place,
if we all showed we cared.
By writing down our special thoughts,
then they could be shared.

Lynn Brown

I 'SMELT TEEN SPIRIT'

I sang along to those melancholy yet sometimes touching lyrics where
melody collided with mayhem
Capturing my life so torn apart and true
I shared in your twisted angst which carved like a knife so deep
and blue
And as a rite of passage and acceptance
I wore those faded beyond repair denim jeans
And those thick coverings of several layers of jumpers and cardigans
with a million fag burns and holes in them at least
And my golden locks of hair I did not comb for endless days on end
And when my world calmed down, I saw myself as an official member
of the lost generation of grunge kids
Clusters of posters of you and your band plastered my outstretched
ceiling to which each rising morning I awoke
And like a new found, instrumental religion I clung upon the immortal
words you preached and spoke
And a spectacular array of magazines, T-shirts and memorabilia that
screamed Kurt Cobain and Nirvana I bought
To me your albums trapped my generation together in the fear of
isolation yet at the same time alone in alienation
I played those ground-breaking albums as an escape, fuelled in the
knowledge I was young and free
I played them constantly, never-tiring back and forth and back and forth
And whilst I like many others entered into the beautiful, atmospheric
syndrome of 'Teen Spirit'
You went on home one cold April day and put the bullet that held the
key to infinity through your confused head
Leaving behind your tortured, draughty cold world unlatched and
undone
And the desperate, destructive sound that to this day stands apart along
with those frightfully cathartic lyrics
I mourned you for awhile but then moved on and left 'Teen Spirit' a
world away in my past

So thank you Kurt for the wicked, mind blowing experience
It's a shame the horizon in your drug-fuelled eyes did not see the vision
of a much bigger picture beyond the mist and fire too.

Saheeda Khan

ALL EMPTINESS IS . . .

Given space, what should I fill it with
the stars that twinkle in the night sky.
To be empty void of reason
tho' it is still not silence.

You are empty,
as a glass on a bar.
Empty is the glass.

Given emptiness,
What should we say it is.
A vacuum?
Lake of oxygen, air, wind or water?

To be within the womb,
as all things are born.
What should I say emptiness is?
Water, liquid, or just space.
Perhaps full rather than empty.

Robert Robb

GM Foods - Friend Or Foe

Geemm (GM) foods and crops
Are they good or bad?
Playing about with our food
Or improving it to stop it going bad?

Toty Tony Blair is unafraid
To eat this geemm food
He thinks those who call it Frankenstein crops
Are being very rude.

Who knows what geemm crops will do
To nature as we know it
But these new crops must have a chance
Or person-kind may blow it!

Banned in schools and from some stores
Will geemm foods really take off?
Or will Joe Public have their way
And tell the Toties to get off.

Who knows what the future may bring
But new ideas must be looked at with stealth
Not banned before we know for sure
What it will do to our health or wealth.

J G Griffiths

GOING SHOPPING

How I like going shopping
seeing all the bargains.
Seeing which one to buy
saying this is a good one to buy.

As I have a glint in my eye on the jumper I like
as I try it on, it seems too small.
As I ask the assistant, have you a larger size
As she turns around, she says, this is the last one I've got
As I leave the shop, very disappointed.

As I go to another shop to get the same jumper
I come away, very disappointed.

I go home and turn to my catalogue
I find the same jumper and place my order.
The operator says one week or two to receive it
I decide I will pop out to the shops.

Next day comes, the jumper arrives
Turns out it's too small.

So with my friends, I send it back, disappointed.

Roger Brooks

THE SINGLE PARENT

I am a single parent
my children are my joy
I have a little girl with rosy cheeks
and a sturdy little boy.

The only sadness that I have
is they will never know a dad.
But even with this handicap
I will see they don't turn bad.

I will work my fingers to the bone
to give them what they need
And hope that when they reach adult age
they both will prosper and succeed.

Lachlan Taylor

AFFLICTED

My greatest sorrow, while this poem I wrote
like a chimney, I puffed and smoked.
My *nicotine craving* took over me.
Smoking tobacco will be the death of me.
Now cancer has claimed my lungs and throat
this terrible feeling, that I will choke.
Some hospital surgeon has operated on me.
While radium treatment withdrew my hair from me.
Never a good life can I hope to live.
My health no power on Earth, can give.
Some day soon, when I am laid to rest.
I feel my poetry writing has past its best.
If only you *smokers* will read and take heed
Only death will come from the dreaded weed . . .

B Marshall

WHAT DOES MY FUTURE HOLD?

What does my future hold?
A crate of gold?
Or am I going to be sitting in the cold?
I don't know!
I wish I did! I usually plan my life ahead.
At least I did, ever since I was a kid!
But now I'm here amid,
My finals of my degree!
Thought it would improve prospects for me !
Even imagined it would hold the key!
But what am I to be?
A graduate with a degree!
What does the future hold!
I haven't yet been told!
I hope I'm not left 'out in the cold'!
I'm looking for a rewarding career!
So I can enjoy it year after year!
Be a success!
I hope. I would guess
But hope alone is not enough.

T Hartley

DUST SETTLES

I see dust sparkle
As a million stars,
Sunlight shining
Through the gap of outside
And the coffee's gone cold now,
On white sheets I let my thoughts drift
Thinking past where thoughts sleep
As music plays without you.
I can close my eyes
Remember candles burning low
Wishing for wishes I wished I'd done.
The sun won't shine forever,
Only the time we're here,
Disappearing behind a cloud
The darkness sets around the room,
With a pause leaves me alone.

Ted Pyman

THE COLOUR I FEEL

Red is my face
the fire in me
red is my anger
and jealousy.
Green is my day
my life and me
green is an apple
my eternal envy.
Yellow is the way
I pale out of sight
yellow is the fear
when I'm alone at night.
Blue is the rain
when it touches me
blue is for coldness
when my heart is empty.

Craig Shuttleworth

Too Many Galaxies In The Sky

Did any one of you people in this world ever
think how many galaxies are flying in the
sky, and none of them come down. Why! Because
God put them up there for a good and important reason.
They have been there for millions of years - Each
one goes around in the sky with exact precision
and with the correct time! And if one
should lose the time everything would fall down!
And the world that we live in will be extinct
forever! But this will never take place because God
is in control of everything! Unless God decides that something
must happen, then nobody can do anything about it!
But even today some experts say to all of us
that this world soon will be struck by an asteroid!
I do not believe it, because God knows better than all
the world experts! They will come down only if God decides!
And, if by a chance one should come to Earth God will push
it out of the earth's way. Enjoy this life, no galaxies or asteroids
will come down from the sky!

Antonio Martorelli

A GOOD IDEA

It's a good idea
To fall in love
It shelters
You from life
Like a kiss
From a dove.
It may be silly,
It may be mad
Love's both of these
And never leaves you sad.

P Allen

HOPE OF THE MILLENNIUM'S DAWN

Dawn creeps over the rim of night
Spreading hope in its rays of light
Hope today man will get it right
Against life's evils they will fight.

A better world is needed for all
Where the good will flourish, the evil fall
Where a childhood is the right of every child
A right to be happy, always ready to smile.

There are resources enough on the Earth
For each to be allowed what they are worth
Enough for every man, woman and child
To live a life not just to survive

Feed the world should not be a dream
With its heads together to devise a scheme
Where surplus of one covers the lack of another
Food for all, every sister and brother.

As the Millennium looms celebrations are planned
Can't we all get together across all the lands
So with the hope of the Millennium blazing dawn
A new world is waiting, a new world is born.

J Lumapak

THE COLOUR RED

The colour red, a hue of fame renown
Reminds this poetess of loving flame.
My heart glows red for love of Jeff, his frown
And smile, his call, I claw like a cat. Did tame.

A red, the shade so deep becomes maroon.
When light, the colour turns to dainty pink.
My favourite tint for ribbons wide, I faint and swoon
As Jeff does pull my hair of curls and wink.

A Pole with eyes of blue and hair of black
Seduced my heart with words of loving tease.
He held me close, his eyes of deep blue-black.
A dance of golden veils for him. Striptease!

Rainbow-hued coloured dance for this man now.
Arousal deep from virgin state.

Sandra A Merlini

WHAT A FRIGHT

Ghosties and ghoulies and long-legged beasties
And all things that go bump in the night.
If you see your wife with a face pack
First thing in the morning it will give you a fright.
Skeletons and spooks that dreaded banshee
Her face with some mud-pack
Will make the bravest man flee.
You will have to stand and stare
Did she have snakes in her hair?
She had cucumber over each eye
Make even the strongest hero cry.
Said this thing is all the rage
Was she starting to show her age.
At the mirror looking at her reflection
Like giving your old wreck its inspection.
She won't be a pin-up star
With something she gets from a jar.

Colin Allsop

CORNISH MEN

Atlantic breakers roll and roar,
Deep from the heart of the ocean floor.
Seagulls wheeling high and free
Over Cornish men on a Cornish sea.

Fishing boats in the early mist,
High on a tide that the sun has kissed,
Follow the winds of eternity
With the Cornish men on a Cornish sea.

The smell of fish in the sheltered bay,
In the ice-cold breath of a winter day.
Then home for a mug of hot sweet tea
Come the Cornish men on a Cornish sea.

Up again with the dawn and away once more,
As their fathers did in the time before.
So it is - and so shall be -
For the Cornish men on a Cornish sea.
So it was - and so shall be,
For the Cornish men on a Cornish sea.

Mavis Joyce Green

DOWN TO EARTH

You are Mother Earth
said he.
In order to win him back
You must become
The Enchantress.

You must suffer
And regain a youthful beauty,
Mysterious fascination.
A power over men
To draw them in.

But do I really want them?
Do I really want
To feel that light
That free?
I wouldn't feel like me!

Give me the security
Of my wide buttocks,
Ample rounded belly
And massive thighs.
At least I will not blow away.

I desire not to be Enchantress
I only want to be me
Plain and ordinary,
Don't want to play the games
Especially not with the likes of he!

Lindsay Chi

BE FREED

A body with muscles and very strong.
A man to be there when things go wrong.
Someone to share and warm the nights.
To kiss and hold, when you turn off the lights.

How often the man turns into a mouse.
He is not there defending the house.
Longing for muscles exploding with steam.
There genetics form like a yellow stream.

Lost in a screen of Arnie or Mel.
Watching them is good and well.
They go home to a life that is real.
For being a woman is what we must feel.

Now females work to keep the bairns fed.
They read them stories and put them to bed.
Often left chanting a spiritual hymn.
Extra strength can be formed in a gym.

Stretching the body and pulling those weights.
They'll be no need to rely on your fates.
A body with muscles and very strong.
You're always there when things go wrong.

Maria Bernadette Potter

A STRANGE SILENCE

The blood it swells and drips on the floor,
I think I am dead though knew not so before
I can no longer see you, your face in my mind,
No longer sense you, this life now behind me -
This blood lies before me, a deep scarlet red
Drenching the sheets of this bloody death bed
And in silence I listen, though fro what, I'm not sure,
I feel myself tiring just waiting for more.
And then you arrive, you stand at my head -
You feel round my wrists, am I alive, am I dead?
You open my eyes, smear blood on my chin
That's warm and sweet and sticks to my skin -
But too late, your eyes a sad smile,
You take hold of my hand and lie down for a while
And here, amidst this strange silence I draw deep
my last breath
And enter the passage, that lead on to this . . .

Tessa Jenkins

DE JURE

There is a truth lurking inside my mind
I have summoned its being to rise up;
To speak out; to explain itself in kind;
To angst over desires I now cup.
Of myself nothing is held from the night
I offer in sways an untold lament
Invariably whether wrong or right
Chancing it bleeds a saddening torment
But this truth is a harvest I must reap
For what good would it be to fester now?
I fear it's better divulged from its sleep
And make a promise by pledging this vow:
Of the untold lurkings inside my mind
To you I'll reveal before we're resigned.

Tony Downing

GUILTY

So they locked him up,
My brother.
Closed the door and turned the key,
On my brother.
Left him there to fret and cry
Left us here to wonder why,
With no thought for you and I
My brother.

So he did wrong,
Did my brother.
Broke the law, went on the run
Did my brother.
Did they stop to question why
Did they see you stand and cry,
Do you know the reason why
My mother?

So now it's time
My brother.
Time to pay for your crime,
My brother.
Did you think we'd leave you there,
Did you think we would not care
Think we'd stand and watch them stare,
You were wrong, my brother.

Shirley Penn

FORSAKEN

You took my love, and changed my life but you never made me
Your wife
You breathed me in and kept me there.
I cherished every moment we shared.
Never in darkness, only shining skies, echoing whispers on,
Love's breath.
Then came the moment, you seized your time.
You walked out the door and left us behind.

Beverley Baker

BE A KID AGAIN? NEVER!

My mum asked me with refrain
Would I want to be a child again?
No I stated firmly and in truth
Children now are fearful and uncouth
No discipline is applied and they shout and demand
I want this or that and are out of hand
They try sex young and take loads of drugs
Smoke early too and pick up partner's bugs
Some get into trouble with the law
Shoplifting, stealing, punch-ups and brawls
Leave home and get into debt
Prostitution to solve problems yet
No thanks to growing up all over again
The trauma, the stress and additional pain.

P Edwards

ME

I had cancer in '93
And I'm still here.
My thoughts and actions have been jumbled
These past few years.
About if and when and am I going to die?

I have cried, 'Why me?' and
Been angry, shouted and screamed,
My family needs me
They are so young and vulnerable.

Could David cope without me?
To hoover, scrub and clean.
The dentist, open days at school

To have an operations was the only solution
But worse was yet to come.

The chemo and radiotherapy were not so nice
The falling out of hair, the sickness did nothing for one's ego.
So I set myself a goal to run the Seven Sisters Marathon.
Which I achieved in the October of '93 and I'm still running on.

This is a shortened version of this poem just for you
So do not be downhearted or feel afraid
For I've gone through hell and back and I'm still here.
Be strong and tough that will bring you through.

So be of good cheer and live every day to the full
And if this touches heart strings and brings tears to your eyes
Just be happy for me and remember this, that Fran is still alive.

Keep smiling.

Fran Doe

FROM BEYOND

I do not want your elegies: my death
Is not some college exercise for rhyme.
Write about *me*. Now, as you draw in breath,
Thank God you knew me, look back on the time
We shared, the precious things of everyday.
Solemnity is not what I desire.
Write this: 'I'll miss his voice, his smile - the way
He'd touch the edges of my life with fire!'
My silence was the only gift I had.
Beyond it lay my love: how could you guess,
On those rare evenings when you found me sad,
That silence was my given power to bless?
Don't think me wise. I had my tigers too;
But it was me they tore: not you.

Jackie Durnin

TELEPHONE FRIEND

We talked in depth, of places we have known
And enjoyed: Like barefoot shores as waves crash in,
Of rustling leaves in the gentle wind,
Wafting scent of meadows newly mown,
And special places near our home,
Where we seek the peace to be found within
The human spirit, to help us win
Strength to go on when we stand alone.

So a friendship began,
I stayed at your place
Chatting long with you and Paul,
Played with Sean and Carol-Ann,
Who had great fun painting my face.
Oh the pleasure I had in seeing you all.

Patrick Allen

UNSEEN BLESSINGS

The void, in which some may believe I dwell,
is contrarily a swim with wonder;
identities merge, then burst asunder -
a myriad entities which then swell,
embracing senses in this private cell,
gifting riches I may sift or plunder -
so do not, please make the standard blunder
and pity these blind eyes I know so well.

Consider, though, how much *you* do not hear,
your terror of accepting helping hand,
the fierce independence which mars each love;
sly false facades so blatant to *my* ear -
jewels you picked which crumbled into sand-
and then . . . and then there's *touch* - more than enough!

Perry McDaid

A SONNET FOR SHAKESPEARE

O Will, they say you were a naughty lad,
poaching deer from Thomas Lucy just for fun.
He was JP which made things twice as bad,
so you left Stratford and went on the run.
In 'drunken Bidford' you were sorely missed
when you cut loose and ran to London town,
for that's when you and all your mates got pissed
while vying for the Bacchanalian crown.
Held horses outside theatres so they say;
after the country life seemed very hard,
but still you gained the skill to write a play
and swiftly you became the nation's bard.
Or could it be that we are all mistaken
and credit you with what belongs to Bacon?

John Callow

THE VIKINGS

Through the low-lying mist veiling the sea
Was glimpsed the prows of dreaded Norsemen's ships.
Panic ensued, villagers turned to flee,
Screams of terror forced from ashen lips;
The husky Vikings splashed towards the shore
Arrogance marking death-defying might.
Odin, mainstay to patriotic core,
Fortified them to fervour for the fight,
Boldly plundering country's meagre wealth
Leaving their genes and language on the way.
Not for them the indignities of stealth
But baying horns beleaguering the fray,
And when Valhalla robbed them of their zest
Set sail into a sunset's tempered rest.

Eileen Shenton

Too Dear

My love, I cannot afford thee anymore.
Thou art too dear for my possessing.
My bonds are taxed for all they're worth,
And my pension? It's depressing.
How can I keep thee? With a Lottery Grant?
Of such riches I'm not deserving.
I have to work to earn my keep -
In MacDonald's I am serving.
I know thou gavest thyself to me,
And thy house and thy four-by-four
So believe me dear, it really hurts
To have to show thee the door,
Please don't say, 'No,' with such intense conviction,
I say, 'Yes.' That means one thing, *eviction!*

Beryl Partridge

INDIFFERENCE

Got up.
Not happy.
Not sad.
Not anything.
Walked out into the road. Did not look. Not aware.
Brakes screeched. Tyres skidded.
Walked on.

Room on the second floor.
Thirty feet up. Concrete below.
Window open. Sat on the ledge.
Nothing moved. Did not go.

Headache. Found pills.
Took two. Stared at the bottle.
How many would . . .
Did not know.

Climbed into bed.
Closed eyes.
Pretend I am dead. Until tomorrow.

Cathy Fleming

THE GEOGRAPHY TEST

Knowledge evades me,
For words I'm at a loss.
I know I must write something,
Albeit a load of dross.
My mind's not in the classroom,
But somewhere far away.
I won't have a GCSE to my name
When I leave this school, someday.
How I long to be successful,
To have a great career,
A car and a house with a garden,
And a holiday three times a year!
Oh, to return to the first year -
To begin with a sparkling clean slate
Always asking for help when I needed it
My homework would never be late.
Detentions would be unheard of -
For praise I'd never yearn.
I'd be on the A/A minus list
At the end of every term.
But I cannot turn the clock back -
Nor can I continue like this -
I feel as though I'm nearing the edge
Of a dark and infinite abyss.
My attention returns to the paper,
On which I've not written a thing -
And the moment I pick up my pen to write,
The end-of-the-lesson bell rings.

Andrea E C Williams

A SIMPLE TEENAGE LOVE

I was never one,
For Miss Saigon,
Or drinking milky tea,
(So what do I find,
To rest my mind,)
But someone the opposite of me.

A quiet, pretty, little girl,
With sticky fingers you did twirl,
Into a monster of Frankenstein,
(Who would growl at teachers,
And dismiss preachers,)
Teenage love, it pushed me out of line.

Jealously and hatred filled,
Once innocent that you have killed,
Can a monster be worse than its creator?
(Exam failure on the certificate,
Absent, absent, late, late, late,)
Rock music loving, Cliff Richard hater.

But then we parted,
No longer half-hearted,
Were the apologies for the scene,
(Sorry Dad, and sorry Mum,
For bad manners and chewing gum,)
From now on I'll keep my bedroom clean.

My first boyfriend was a blast,
But I'd rather he stayed in the past,
Don't worry now, that beast has gone,
(Back to good grades,
As the old me fades,)
But only until I get another one!

Angela Claire Jones

POET'S THOUGHTS

What makes the poet to be know
Far as the country extends.
Make the remotest person his friend.
His work he counts but as the wind
Sometimes wronged, sometimes sad,
Uttering nothing, but sheltered words of love
Writing happiness is his words.
That light upon a far off shore
Sometimes a wandering star.
Water in the deserts, oceans, near and far
A tree that looks so tall
The sun, fair and shining
The weary, the aged, the grief
the anger,
May all find and cast it away.
It is that I seek it, with nothing to hide
Inspired by truths, that some may fear.
My soul with happiness and goodness overflows.
It would be that which well I write
and love.
Fresh of the mind
my answer to
Shakespeare.

P Carvell

SUPER HOG

Prickles was there when his mother died.
Sat waiting at the kerbside.
He watched as his mother became flat,
Transformed into a backdoor mat.
He was absolutely gutted, so was she,
A hedgehog abandoned and alone was he.
His spines were limp; his eyes were wet,
He felt in need of a jolly good vet.

He returned to his home, which had always been nice,
And brooded as he nibbled on worms and woodlice.
Prickles was angry and sad at the loss of his mum,
Which made him determined his time would come.
Out with the punch bag, put on some weight.
He was to alter the world and the hedgehog's fate.
He pumped up the iron. Had a diet of snails,
'Til has muscles were firm and his spines were like nails.
Super Hog was born. He left his safe abode,
With a mean and savage squint he set off for the road.

He trembled as he waited; he must not get 'cold feet',
For he knew that revenge would taste really sweet.
He marched from the verge; his spines stuck up high,
'Okay, you punk, this is where you say goodbye.'
There was a bang and a hiss and it shot past his head,
As it skidded to a halt he believed the squashing machine dead.
He was a buzz of excitement, although his heart still had pain,
So that is why Super Hog. killed again and again.
You see,
He was there when his mother died.
Sat waiting at the kerbside.

Marlene Parmenter

WE WHO MOCK

We who mock the dinosaur
had best take care.
He is not lost but gone before
and furthermore
he went unwillingly,
not of his own accord.

But we poor human fools,
think we can break all rules.
We'd best beware!
Our meddling with this world is chillingly
inept. We can't afford
to be complacent. Before long,

although we think we're strong
and that the rest of nature's weak
and subject to our will,
we'll find it's not the case.
It is the human race
that's nearly run.

But still,
some other creature, one that's meek
will be the one
to inherit once we've whimpered off.
Oh, you may scoff!
If pygmy shrews will one day rule the earth so be it.
I only hope *they* know a good thing when they see it!

Chris Gutteridge

VE DAY

For peace in our time,
In unwavering line,
Shoulder to shoulder,
None were bolder.
Fearful yet brave,
As wave after wave,
They fell on the plain.
Not even the rain
Could wash away,
The pain on display,
Of those faces that day.
They gave it a name,
Of sorrowful fame.
On the eighth day of May,
Remember this day!
A plane soars high,
Like a bird in the sky.
The war is won,
But for each mother's son,
And daughter too,
Who died for the freedom of me and you.
No greater love.
And the plane above
Flies a victory roll,
For one and all,
Who answered the call.

Anne Marie Birley

REPEATS

I was scanning through the TV Times
just the other day,
And thinking of the licence fee
that I had got to pay,
And as I turned the pages
to see the programmes there,
I suddenly realised as I sat
there in my chair.
The film that I was watching
had been shown the year before.
So I looked through all the pages
of that magazine to see
how many repeated programmes
were to be on my TV
And when I saw that half the things
had been on my screen before,
I thought,
it doesn't seem quite right to me
I ought to pay only half the fee,
but I'm sure the BBC won't stand for that
So would you mind if I came round with a hat.

Rita Webster

WHY?

Feed me Sir for I am hungry
And my feet are cold and sore
I have no time for you beggar girl
My train is running late and I must go

Please clothe me Sir for I am cold
And my coat is ragged and torn
Away from me women and feed yourself
My supper is getting cold

Help please Sir I am ill and dying
And I have no room to sleep in
Get off the floor and get a job girl
I'm fed up with paying for you lot

She has died Sir out here in the rain
Her frail body covered in bruises and dirt
Her father beat and raped her
Now who will look after her child?

C Skilton

PUT US OUT OF THEIR MISERY

I say give the druggies an overdose
Rid society of these ghosts
White faced
Staring eyes
With needle holes in arms and thighs

Crime rate's high
Thief and murderer is let loose
As craving's so strong it makes its own noose.

When tourniquet is tight
And the craving is fed
They then revert to the living dead
I say give the druggies an overdose
Rid society of these ghosts.

Susan Lewis

REQUIEM

The last sad cleric
Hunched at his desk
Despairs over the words
Of another pointless text.

The belief long passed
Tucked away in books
Stolen from our minds
As time steals looks.

The cleric now rises
For God's last stand
Preaching his final sermon
To a barren land.

Echoing around the church
Where no one worships
His voice then falters
Fading thru' trembling lips.

One more prayer offered
We heathens shan't hear
Our hearts closed forever
The end is near.

The church in ruins
The cleric has died
Just like our beliefs
The tombs now hide.

John Marshall

Auf Weidersehen An' A' Tha'

We reached our destination
At a second rate hotel,
We had an inclination
That we had arrived in Hell.
They only could speak German
On an island next to Spain,
Palma, in Mallorca,
We may never go again.

Germans at the swimming pool
And Germans at the bar,
But the Germans at the diner
Were taking things too far,
A continental breakfast was
A brick roll with some cheese,
I believe I would have ate some
Bar for the mould on these.

So sangria and German beer
Was the order of the day,
We went through two weeks of this,
We were glad to *get away.*

Timothy Alexander

ROAD WORTHY

Every day, it's sad to say, a lot of people die,
driving down the motorway it's easy to see why.
Vehicles of every kind go from lane to lane,
without a thought for what's behind, they turn right back again.

A motorway is not a track to speed along at will,
and little children in the back, should not be there to kill.
And even on a normal road you need to be aware,
that if your car you overload a greater load you'll bear.

Think before you take a drink before you hit he road,
and maybe if you stop and think you'll never overload.
You need the speed to hit the brake before you hit the wall,
and if you're only half awake, you shouldn't drive at all.

Signs are there for you to see the danger that's ahead,
so drive with care and then you'll be alive instead of dead.
And when you're out don't fool about but drive with skill and pride,
for if you don't there is no doubt that Satan thumbs a ride.

Remember when you're at the wheel and driving with concern,
Jesus can be very real and help you in return.
For He is there as One who knows what you are all about,
but when you see how fast it goes that's when the Lord gets out . . .

John R Seville

EASTER SONG

Christmas was a happy time,
We sang of the Saviour's birth.
From every church the bells did chime
Resounding o'er the earth.

But then Good Friday came along
And full of sadness was our song.
Our Lord upon the cross did die
To save the souls of you and I.

On Sunday, what a joyous cry
Was heard; our Jesus rose on high,
No more entombed in earthy grave
For us He came our souls to save.

And as we pray on Easter Day
And in the church our flowers lay
Aloud we sing the well known hymns
To Jesus Christ, our Saviour King.

Inez M Henson

DECLINE AND FALL

Hush, hush the people are asleep
Their sleep is terminal - and
Seemingly without redress,
And for the dead, none left to weep.

Lost empire holds a cloak of shame
Imposed by those above, so sadly born
Bereft of pride, close love
Of land of greatest fame.

Hush, sleep on, as all is lost
And piece by piece, your value
Is plucked away by alien hands;
They reach for all, all to our cost.

Sleep while betrayal squanders wealth
On lesser nations, powered to take
Our assets, earned with blood
Then, stolen by a foreign stealth.

And, those above, those left to lead
The very ones from down below
Who step aloft by breaking every fence
Forgetting on the way our nation's need.

Our laws are made a mockery, by they
Across the channel, of once defence,
Our would-be masters, to whom
Our leaders all commands obey.

Henry J Green

CIVILISATION

Tearing down industrialisation
With every cut-back, every trick,
Tearing down civilisation
Brick by brick.

Profit and loss misinformation
New speak, economy downturns,
Politicians fiddle like Nero
While Home burns

Tearing down, restructualisation
Selling us out, increasing tax,
Who gives a toss if this once proud nation
Is pole axed.

Closures, rationalisation,
Job losses, another big stick
To tear down civilisation
Brick by bloody brick.

Alma J Harris

THE VILLAGE

The church bell tolls, the village sleeps,
The cockerel calls at dawn,
The sheep are grazing on the hills
And lambs seem all forlorn.

Thatched roofs, just like a chocolate box,
Nestle within the hills;
Gardens hum with bees and birds
And butterflies add thrills.

The farmers wend their weary way,
They toil both day and night;
Their tractors plod along the lanes,
They are an awesome sight.

The village hall, the Post Office,
The corner shops abound;
The postman calls with vital mail,
He has a busy round.

The pubs, the ducks, the sheep-dogs
Add beauty to this land;
This heritage that comes to us
Is God's almighty hand.

The millennium will come to pass,
The village will remain,
And just as in the time of Christ,
The shepherd's crook is plain.

Beryl Owen

SCONES AND SCONES

My mother looked like the Queen . . .
Until she was 50.
But she didn't talk like the Queen thank heavens.
Neither did I,
Until grammar school stepped in my way.

Pointlessly middle class.
Petite Bourgeoisie.
And I learnt to know 'jolly'
'Good gosh and golly'
Which had no real meaning as far as I could see.

My mother talked like an English girl.
With her chin up
From Southsea to Canterbury,
With no accent to pick up or slip up.

I didn't have an accent.
I had all inflictions under the sun.
Pick a pronunciation
For any situation,
Buh I ain' nevuh gon' choose jus' one.

Susannah Denimn

BRITISH SPIRIT

Each country has a spirit,
Each nation its own way,
Each place has its people,
A soul that with it stays.

No matter what we have no more,
The pound, the Royals, the meat,
Our England has her spirit,
That stays beneath our feet.

Our monarchs may seem old to others,
Our meat may seem so plain,
Our pound, a pointless difference,
But our country's magic stays the same.

Each country has a spirit,
Each nation its own way,
No matter what they take from us,
Our spirit stays the same.

Karina Lickorish

IN A PERFECT WORLD

Across the field it hangs there, beauty I can see,
the colours of a rainbow, that God has given me.
A field so full of flowers, the smell it is untrue.
And over there an old oak tree, but close by something new.
A baby deer so feeble, he stumbles across the ground,
as his mother she calls to him, for some fresh grass she has found.
A perfect world that I can see before my very eyes,
but knowing what the real world is, I turn and say goodbye.

Vicki Michele Loveday

HOME

What does it mean, this word, this place
To me a fire, Mum's smiling face
Workers on bicycles passing by
Good smells from the oven like
Mum's apple pie.

Green privet hedges none can compare
The factory's whistle
Its piercing blare.
Double-deckers, fish and chip shops
Dancing Saturdays at local hops.
Rosy-cheeked children going to school
Mothers with prams at park paddling pools.
The local pub and the landlord's pleas
In his friendly voice
'Time, gentlemen please!'

To some these things mean nothing at all
Probably seem insignificant and small.
To me, this word, this place, is home
Dear England just across the foam.

Melville Lomax

GREAT BRITAIN FOR ME

Where else can you get food
that tastes so good?
Cornish pasties, Devon cream teas,
all readily for me to please.
Haggis from bonnie Scotland,
Soda bread from the Emerald Isles,
Bara Brith from Wales,
English fish and chips,
Pie and mash, faggots and peas,
all available with ease.

What other nation,
can give such elation,
During every spring,
listen to the birds that sing.
Songs sung so sweetly,
from the tops of every tree.
What more can be said,
as the golden daffodils nod their heads.
Early morning dew, each day anew,
bright and fresh for me and you.

Where else can a variety of spoken word,
be so widely heard?
Sweet is the Welsh tongue,
handed down for so long,
Celtic Irish, lilting Cornish,
Broad Scottish, Queen's English.
Dialects from each county,
all unites us in one country.
This island surrounded by sea
will always be ideal for me.

Elaine Andrea Hicklin

BRITAIN IT'S GREAT

The Silver Ghost Rolls,
Michael Owen's goals.
Ben Sherman collars,
Pounds instead of dollars

Lennox Lewis' punch,
A traditional ploughman's lunch,
A pint of real ale,
A Canterbury tale.

Robbie William's hits,
The East End in the Blitz,
A Constable country scene,
Her Majesty the Queen.

Andrew Lewis

FISHING BOATS

Is there any old fishermen
who could still tell a tale
of their time at sea,
of when the fishing fleet
set sail
out of harbour to catch
the silver herrings in the
North Sea?
Is there anyone left
who still remembers
standing on the quay
to wave them goodbye
to welcome them home again
at the end of the day?
Once there were many
fishing boats as far as
the eye could see
bringing home their catch
of silver herrings
fresh from the sea.

K Lake

LOVE OR FRIENDSHIP?

I have a new girlfriend
but she doesn't yet know.
I would like to tell her so,
but she is only my friend.
I don't want to make it the end.
How to let her know, that I love her so?
What sort of message to send?
If I tell her now, I could end up sad,
for all the feelings built up inside.
I don't want to sit around and hide,
but is it the right thing to do?
To lose everything between us would be bad,
All I need to say is, 'I love you.'

Alex Harrison (14)

CHURCH BELLS OF ST MARY'S, BEDDINGTON

Hundreds of years on the Lord's day
Bells have called to praise and pray
On Sunday morning hear the sounds
Of ancient church bells, ringing rounds
Bursting from the tower of stone
Masking all the traffic's drone.

Dusty belfry, steep cold stairs
On practice night who sees or cares
When ringers pull the sallies bright
And pealing bells ring through the night.
London, Stedman, Norwich, dodging up and down
Mathematical pattern of Plain Hunt floats above the town.

Hear joyful chime of wedding bells
And doleful toll of funeral knells.

Our church bells are our English tongue
And endless changes can be rung
From John O Groats down to Land's End
Our church bells loud, their message send.

Valerie Coleman

QUIRKY

We are quaint and quirky
      Go out in the midday sun
To foreigners we're very strange
      We are English every one.

Who thought of steam engine
      Who invented the jet
Where did Shakespeare come from
      I haven't finished yet.

Where did the Beatles come from
      Andrew Lloyd Webber too
And don't forget the Spice Girls
      They are English through and through.

Who stood up to Hitler
      Who won two world wars
Thank God for little England
      The world owes us applause!

Fred Magan

MEMORIES

Mother, her warm breath
On my baby cheek
Her comforting arms
When I felt weak.
After childish tiffs
Mother's advice I'd seek,
Teenage dates, home late
Up the stairs, not that creak!
Mother's light going out
But never, never, would she peek;
Then comes the time
For a job to seek,
Mother's stalwart love is there
So to her the news I leak:
Mum! I've done it! Got the job!
Her shining pride makes me meek:
Love you Mum.

Jasmine Dienes-Stevens

WHAT AM I TO DO?

What am I going to do, when I have to leave you standing there?
I've tried to lose my heart just so I wouldn't care,
but it's no good, the thoughts haunt me at night,
without you with me darling, I've no future in my sight.

You see, I've only lived for the times we shared together,
I've always prayed that they would 'be' forever,
but goodbye has come around again, the word fills me with pain,
what do I do now, without you I'll go insane.

I'll go insane because my world will cave in around me,
everything we went through together will surround me,
your lovely kind voice, your sunny smiling face,
now that you are gone, my world is an empty place.

What am I to do?
I only ever wanted to stay with you,
all the material things in the world, I would trade,
if I could remain with you,
you've been my world and all I've needed to survive,
now I'm having to say goodbye to my reason for staying alive.

Claire J Young

OPINIONS, OPINIONS

Girls on boys, boys on girls,
Thinking about them makes my head go in twirls.
I like boys sometimes, but they can be mean.
Hanging around with girls just isn't my scene.
Some girls I hang with are alright
I try to fit in with all my might.
My best friends are Nick and Stu,
I can fit in with them, whatever I do.
I play soccer and kerbs, I run too!
I like being a tomboy, I don't know why,
It's better, I suppose, than being shy.

Joanne Shields

MOTHER EARTH

Old Mother Earth puts on a coat
Ermine white of wintry snow
As she is pregnant with new life
Dormant in her bowels below

But she reveals a brighter side
Whilst giving birth in spring
Appearing in a flowery look
With life awakening

Then promise of the early blossom
Matures to summer ripeness
Bounty of our Mother Earth's
Gift of fruitfulness

Time comes then for her autumn wear
A coverlet instead
Painted bright with ageing leaves
In shades of brown and red.

Thus in ever-changing mood
Mother Earth will nurture us
Through seasons of our little lives
Until the time for exodus.

Jack Cash

THE MANOR HOUSE

The manor house stood quiet and still,
The lake of blue was placid.
No chimney smoke the air did fill.
No children's happy laughter.

A scent of roses filled the air
Beside an old rustic seat,
The bridge that spanned the lake so fair,
Echoed no pattering feet.

Within the house a stillness reigned
Till sometimes it was broken,
By gentle ghosts who came, and deigned,
To haunt a beloved realm.

Margaret Knox Stubbs

PICCADILLY CIRCUS

It's an aerial view,
You can't see me
But I can see you.

It's a busy place,
Everyone, every day
In this human rat race.

Your Fosters, TDK and Panasonic;
Your Coca-Cola, McDonald's and Schweppes
Are this city's tonic.

Down the subway to the underground,
Everyone, everywhere on the move,
Even the traffic goes round and round.

But the London Pavilion is for me;
For this is an aerial view of people
Walking the streets of Piccadilly.

Marcus Tyler

GOODBYE

Down the shallow cheeks,
A tear runs from his eye,
As he remembers yesterday,
When to his wife he said goodbye.

Goodbye to one he truly loved,
And still does to his day,
He loved her many years ago,
When first her eyes he met.

Then down his withered face,
A tear runs from his eye,
As he remembers yesterday,
When to his beloved wife he said 'Goodbye.'

S Barjona

THOUSAND YEARS

erich von daniken said
return to the stars
one said today we
cannot even go anywhere
that is distant space
the costs of space travel
hold back any progress
in a thousand years
from this nineteen ninety nine
what will be there
to call of space travel
if the same things apply
no the huge cost
bore by the masses
it is not right
no it never is
it's all right for
the big clever ones
to insist on what
they think is right
we are all earthbound
tied to the earth
you leave it only
at great context of risk
it's not so normal
for to exist in a
thing that is weightlessness
no the body has to
adjust to all the conditions
it can wear one out

Richard Clewlow

SMILE

Such a shocking smile,
I'd like it to stay for a while,
You're a lovely thing
Because you always bring
Light into the night,
Breathe when you're close to death,
You'll always be the light in my eyes,
You make me hear all the cries,
Cries of laughter,
And then after,
Cries which seem real,
Because we know how you feel,
The memory stays true,
How could we go on without you?

Tracey Rush

JIGSAW PUZZLES, TOY BALLOONS AND BALLS IN THE AIR

Life is like a great jigsaw puzzle
That we try and piece together,
And none of us know
What the finished picture will look like.

We assemble and scramble
We build up an image,
And then destroy it again
By our impatience for the future.

Life is like so many toy balloons
We float around, full of hot air,
Blown by the wind of our imaginings
Lacking direction, and a purpose in life.

We float skyward and down again
Inflating and deflating,
Living a punctured life
With no substance at all.

Life is like so many balls in the air
We juggle and conjure,
And see the pretty colours
But colour blindness sets in
And we let them fall again

Life's toys can become banana skins
When we try to grab them all,
We must learn patience and humility
Or else our lives are in free fall

And we are left
With nothing at all.

Ian Barton

THE PRIDE OF DIANA

She walked with grace
And talked with ease
A flower that bloomed
All year round
But that flower died
And the world cried
Yes we can carve her
Name with pride

She loved everyone around
Her
No matter what colour or
Creed
She sat with people with terrible
Diseases
And gave her heart away
Yes Diana
We carve your name today.

Her life was not perfect
But had a lot to give
She rests in peace now
What would her life have been
If she had lived.
Now she is in Heaven
With God by her side,
Yes Diana
We carve your name with
Pride.

Pauline M Wardle

MY SISTER

Sisters can be very nice
and very bossy too
I have a sister just like that
but what am I to do.
Sometimes she makes me happy
Other times she makes me sad
But my sister has a heart of gold
Even though she gets me mad.
But deep down, we are really close
I wouldn't trade her for another
I just wish, she'd stop nagging
Me as if she was my mother.

A Whyte

WINTER

Winter months are long and dreary,
Dark clouds with gale force winds,
Torrential rain, and hailstones
Beating hard against the window panes.
Thunderstorms, ice and snow,
Children sledging, playing
Snowballs, praying that the snow
Won't go.
When at last the fun is over,
And the thaw begins.
Rivers overflow, high tides
Sweep over the promenade.
Streets of houses, fields are
Flooded.
People wondering where for
Safety - can they go.
From behind the clouds, sometimes
The sun appears, radiantly putting
On a show.
How I long for the springtime
When the flowers start to grow.
Trees in full blossom, swaying
Gently to and fro:
Birds will sing in their nests,
Watching their eggs, hatch one by one.
The green sweet smelling grass,
Winter will soon go.

Doreen Petherick Cox

Psalm Of Light

The Lord is my lantern, I shall not falter
He goes before me on the dark and lonely footpaths.
He lifts the shadows that wait around my door
He lights the empty corners of my room.
In the greyness of doubt and uncertainty,
He will guide me.
In the darkness and hurt and despair
I shall seek his brightness.
His light is constant and is comfort everlasting.
I shall travel with him always
And he will lead me, safely on the
Journey of my life.

William Price

THE DEMOLITION OF FORT WHITEROCK, WEST BELFAST

Fort Whiterock's now rubble
A pile of the past
But will British oppression
Be withdrawn at last?

No. A Union Jack
Is still marring the view
The taxes are British
The troops, they are too

The dust that was raised
As each building came down
Was intended to block out
The glint from the crown

But the cheers from the public
All shouting 'Hurray!'
Are their prayers that soon Britain
Will be on her way.

Kim Montia

CONTROL?

Are we individuals, or
Product made?
Have the workers all been
Paid? The sun comes
Up and then it
Falls. Like the man who has
It all.
Like a chain around our
Foot we're
Forced to walk the wrong way
Accepting as the truth, what
The media has to say
Have the lessons we learnt
Taught us too less
Can we decide
For ourselves what's
Right, wrong or best?
How much control
Do we have?

Ben Seymour

THE DYING STARS

How close they are!
Above the tree line to the west -
so want of spring,
That in this chilling wind,
seems so afar!
But one is not a star!
The lower of the two . . .
Twinkling in the blue - darkening;
It will not stay!
But beams full bright!
Until the sun has said . . . 'Goodnight'
While all alone -
the colder light will stay -
then go his way -
mourning!
Now that she is gone.

Tom Ritchie

THE SNAPSHOT

Just an ordinary snapshot
of a friend at the seaside
except the intrusive
chap in the background.

It's quite good of Sally
yet I scarcely see her
so much am I drawn to
that figure all alone.

He didn't spoil the picture
hesitating in shadows
by that warning notice
of dangerous cliffs.

I don't think that he fell,
there was no commotion
and nothing in the news -
but I do think he jumped.

Geraldine Bruce

ON OR OFF?

On or off?
Finger on button signals direction
Whether all watched or careful selection,
A godsend for anyone confined to bed,
Leisure or education at once outspread.

An option
To the frail or lonely abandoned on isle
In front seats of arenas, theatres, awhile,
Amid crowds cheering no more an exile.

A choice;
Balanced viewing inset into one's realm,
Cannot overtake when one's at the helm
Returning from work taut and tense from day's stress
Relax with the box, slowly decompress

The children
Can learn with programmes of their own
Enlightening minds, or fantasising with zones,
One to one instruction, even when alone.

Television,
The eighth wonder of the world when reviewed
What knowledge, illuminations accrued,
Most of mankind has benefit of TV;
Prior we were purblind to countries oversea.

Awareness,
Understanding different people, creeds,
Poverty, starvation, realising their needs,
Available day or night a boon indeed!

Hilary Jill Robson

SHE AND THE SEA

I've seen you breathing
out over an angry sea
with your hair being whipped
by the wind's salty spit

stinging eyes to red
cherry lips to blue
hands to bright white
claws gripping railings.

Earth's spry fury
met with new vigour,
as your stern smile
taunts its flagrancy.

Gulls fight the gale
tipping and sliding
through air pockets
with natural maladroit

while fish hurtle
with the undercurrent.
No rock will survive
this constant abuse,

no tree holds its ground
to offer midday shade.
No, your defiant gaze
out upon the sea's spasms

will surely shift continents
and shake churches' steeples
ringing the greened bells
to the pavement's cracks.

Men hide themselves
in self-appointed importance
steering rusty ships
to catch nature's bounty

without avowing your stare.
This raped land yearning
for some justice,
some reason for its state.

So your sympathetic tears
mix salt and salt together
capsizing rescue boats
full of gentlemen.

Andy Mcpheat

BAD HABITS?

During the day, when I have a moment,
Or two or three or four,
I like to watch my TV set
And bolt across the door.

I find it educating and entertaining too,
Especially in the afternoon,
When there's nothing else to do.

I'm partial to soap opera and cookery galore
And sometimes in the evenings,
I'll watch a little more.
I wouldn't be without it, not one insy-winsy bit,
I'd miss my six part dramas, they really are a hit.

I can't wait for digital and more programmes besides,
I'll still be watching in December,
When you're singing your Yuletides.

I know I sound obsessive, now, don't get in a fret,
I just can't help myself, I love my TV set!

Paula Burlinge

THERE'S A TRUER VISION THAN TV

If God invented television,
I'm sure there'd be no obscenity
Broad-minded is too dangerous.
Songs of praises to bore all faithless ones.

Man invents in modesty
Human nature will explore,
Beyond what's good or best,
There's no telling people how to live,
Example is the greater one.

The fight for good goes right on
It's in us all, and there for all,
Temptation vast and curiosity,
Ever tempting all human weaknesses
In a world of worldliness
The truest visions comes from on high
In all humbleness.

Rachel Taylor

ON THE BOX
(Dedicated to Afifa and Fahad)

Television too is a wonderful invention.
Life is varied, colourful and colourless as well
which can be reached to every person
as each land is trying that.
Each child should be literate and numerate.
Personal direct face to face communication
is gradually fading.
As each person after work
and looking after the house
does not have so much time,
and money to go to each person's home
which is encouraged by the presence of telephone.
Open University is in existence,
it will let every viewer/person to explore
what I have within me.
To explore . . . to develop . . . and entertain
and to choose from it what I want.
I am really interested and concerned.
What I indeed want to do.
It can make every person think.
What I want and
what I am contributing.
So no person should moan and groan
about anything . . . everything.

Ghazanfer Eqbal

THE GRAVE

Every day we pass the gravestone.
A grey grave with a weather-beaten face,
I wonder.
I wonder who lived before.
Someone who laughed,
someone who cried,
someone who lived,
someone who died,
and as I see my kids
scurry through the stones,
like the squirrels,
I smile. A strange contrast?
Death seems a lifetime away,
and we move swiftly on.

A M Craxford

ON THE BOX

I remember early days,
Days of pleasant disbelief.
At the modern miracle
Fast becoming Leisure's thief.

All the family, lost in wonder,
For a few hours every day
Muffin - Annette Mills - The Flintstones,
Yogi Bear - no time for play.

Often in the midst of programmes,
My small son was in despair,
Power-drilling broke the picture,
Early learning, (how to swear).

I have known him dash outside then,
Fearful for his programme's sake,
Knocking, pushing neighbours' doorbells,
Pleading for a respite break.

Since those days our modern wonders
Have eliminated much distress,
Digital, or disc and cable, helped
To end such youthful stress.

When I ponder those beginnings,
Day and night the box aglow,
My nostalgia is for programmes,
Which we used to value so.

Nowadays it's sex and violence,
Punctuating night and day.
Even more the 'Thief of Time' that
Dominates - no time for play

Still a boon for many people,
Invalid, ill and feeble too,
Housebound, helping their affliction,
Giving them a 'point of view'.

Leonard T Coleman

A Day With TV

Daytime TV was never for me,
But since being ill now it has to be,
The first of the day is the Kilroy debate,
This man has a brain that is really great.

The following chat show is a waste of space,
It makes my mind boggle and my heart start to race,
I need stimulation to occupy my mind,
So when choosing a channel it can be a right bind!

I don't care for sport, it bores me to tears,
I just close my eyes and cover my ears,
It should be on one channel for the fans to see,
And leave space for programmes for people like me!

I follow the soaps without a thought in my head,
Sometimes left wondering what somebody said!
The afternoon film can be good or bad,
Making you smile or leaving you sad.

The evening arrives with the local news,
Followed by a programme wanting your views.
Then an hour of soaps followed by 'The Bill',
And a look at the clock, another hour to fill!

The day has flown by and what have I learned,
When for stimulation I've sat and yearned?
I'm away to my bed to open a book,
And maybe tomorrow watch 'Ready Steady Cook'!

Joan M Crow

QUANTUM DREAMING

There is a place where I go
At night when I'm asleep;
I sometimes fly or just appear
In this vast realm so deep,
This is a world where I can do
Exactly as I please,
Live out all desires with simplicity
And ease,
All I see, touch and feel such reality
Profound,
While knowing that I'm in my bed with
Eyes so tightly bound.
I have another power a faculty to see,
Transcending all the past disguise of
What I thought was me.
In that vast sleeping realm the things
I touch and feel
With clear alert awareness that all of
It is real.
As solid as the waking world in which
I spend each day,
Deluded by the senses there in much the same sad way.
To choose between these two vast realms
And call one true or fake,
Can never say to me in truth if I'm
Asleep or I'm awake.
To pick out one of these vast realms
To call reality, would rest upon
What I perceive reality to be.

Bradford Owen Fatooros

THE PARANORMAL

The paranormal? Oh yes! It exists
I have definite proof of this!
Year ago, I had a nightmare
That truly raised the roots of my hair,
I saw a man fall, hammer in hand,
Who, as he fell said, 'Oh my God' and
I woke to the snap of his back at 4.00am
I called my husband, there and then,
Who, very boldly cried 'Shut up you're dreaming,'
And went back to sleep, leaving me steaming.
The next night, at dinner I scanned 'The News'
And there, front page, was the news
Of a man and a fatal accident at Brighton
While fixing loud speakers to the 'Pavilion'.
The man concerned was my brother-in-law
And I'd seen it all happen *the night before.*

Winifred M Swann

FANTASY

I am waiting for you
As the twilight falls over the hill
I feel and sense the heather on the moor
Now I see you in the distance
Riding so nobly as you always do
You are dismounting
For our horses will stay together
As you and I will do the whole night through.
I am wearing my dress of lavender and lace
You are in your military, your tunic of red and gold
I run to you for you are my beloved one
Oh! see a button from your jacket fall to the floor
Let it be my talisman forever more.
We kiss we talk for hours on end
For you are not only my lover, you are my friend.
All night long your hands caress me
Your lips never lift from mine.
And now the morning dew falls upon my crumpled gown
It is almost light
Yet your kisses are still warm upon my mouth.
It's true came
The battle did not take you as they said
That it is only fantasy inside my head
That you will come no more, that you are dead
But I can recall every word you said
And your talisman rests warm and safe within my palm
For it proves you really came to me.
My love! My soul! My heart!
Am I left with just your memory
And the faint sound of a reverie?

D Brook

MY CHANCE TO DREAM

I'm neither old nor bold in my dreams
And awaken smothered in sweat
Wherever I go I'm chased by a foe
It's never-ending and goes on yet.

Who my enemy is, I can't figure out
And have no idea what it's all about
   It's a relief to awake
   Then a deep breath to take
   Hoping tonight, that they'll give me a break.
What a surprise to open my eyes
It's all quiet on the sleeping front.

D S Hussey

DYING HEART

Through my bedroom window last night
a fairy flew in and caused me such a fright.
She was tired and weary and had lost her way
and asked me so sweetly if she could stay.

She lay on my bed right next to me
her colourful wings spread out so prettily.
I woke up early the very next day
and found she had flown away.

Was it a dream? Had she really been here?
Then I saw on the bed so bright and clear,
a ring of dust left from her wings
glowing like jewels fit for kings.

Magic dust to make my heart strong
so I can play and dance for which I so long.
Maybe one day she will visit me again
now that my heart is no longer in pain.

Carole Hoy

MY DREAM - MY HOPE

I have a dream - I am by living waters and they
are flowing free - in this dream there are ways of peace -
no harm is taking place - and man is walking the earth free of fear -
in this dream no shadows of death appear - only skies of endless
happiness before the eyes - is this just a thought - a dream as
it has its foundations based on the Holy Book - the Bible known
to man - Amen.

Rowland Patrick Scannell

NIGHTMARES

I received a postcard from my Aunt Alice,
A beautiful picture of the Assumption of our Lady
I believe hangs in Buckingham Palace.
In sleep my subconscious turned the event into a parody
Of horror. As I relate what my dream enacted
I have always been in awe of Alice's beauty and wit,
Especially reading her comments of this wonderful trip.
She wrote how wonderful she felt gliding
Gliding down the ballroom stairs, almost sliding,
But not quite fulfilled without a ball gown.
She always had a smile or audible quip, rarely a frown.
In my horror of this traumatic subconscious dream
I saw my aunt gliding down towards me. Long black hair,
Pouting lips, her attire black, far too black for her,
A microphone held in her hand as she held sway.
Fishnet stockings, she was Cher for a day.
As she began to sing 'I've got you babe'
Her head suddenly tumbled from her torso,
Which like a football bounced down step by step.
As she concluded her song, torso still erect,
I awoke trembling, absolutely drenched in sweat.

J Baker

MY CUPIDITY

In a dream I discovered Aladdin's Lamp
And rubbed it vigorously.
A genie appeared in a puff of smoke
With a promise of wishes three.
Not wanting to waste just one precious wish
Through wishing too hastily,
I took some time in making my choice
From a rather long litany.

'In my wildest dreams,' I said at last,
'I've wished for prosperity,
Living a life into ripened, old age,
E'en longer than longevity;
And finding a place, wherever it lies,
Where nothing but harmony.
I'm sure I would bask in such ultimate bliss
If these were a certainty.'

'In your wildest dreams!' the genie then laughed.
'You're wishing that these came to be?'
Again came his laugh both lengthy and loud,
Ringing out boisterously.
'Strange how most mortals will wish for the same
To further their felicity.
So be it then, your wishes shall soon
Become a reality.'

El Dorado itself rendered gold for my taking,
No longer an old fantasy.
I settled in Shangri La to ensure
My own immortality.
Discovered through these Utopian gifts, -
Complete tranquility.
And never considered, or once gave a thought,
To my cupidity.

Yes, all of my wishes, en bloc, came to pass,
But only in dreams, don't you see.
For that is the way you maybe recall
Genie's promise was made unto me.
As for his laugh, so loud and so long,
No longer a mystery.
I now know the truth why the genie had laughed.
He had laughed at the joke upon me.

Mary Ryan

ANTHONY

Thank you for loving me that special way you do.
Your love is such a precious gift,
That I know I am truly blessed!
You show so much compassion and kindness,
That's only known from a Saint.
You are always so attentive, loving, caring and understanding.
Your hugs swallow me up and embrace my soul,
Your tenderness touches my heart and makes me weep,
Your patience is such a virtue.
You are an amazing person,
I feel so privileged to know you,
Yet alone to be loved by you!
I will treasure your love forever.
I will ensure our love blossoms,
And is never left to wither.
I've found my special true love in you,
And I'm never going to let you go.

Yours forever
Kim

Kim Rands